Waypoints

by

JOHN DELANEY

ISBN 978-0-912887-51-7

Library of Congress Control Number: 2017940520

Cover and Interior Design by Lauren Grosskopf

Pleasure Boat Studio books are available
through your favorite bookstore
and through the following:
SPD (Small Press Distribution) Tel. 800-869-7553
Baker & Taylor 800-775-1100
Ingram Tel 615-793-5000
Amazon.com and bn.com

and through
PLEASURE BOAT STUDIO: A LITERARY PRESS
www.pleasureboatstudio.com
Seattle, Washington

Contact Lauren Grosskopf, Publisher
Email: Lrslate88@gmail.com

For Jo

The cover image of a windrose comes from the 1492 portolan chart of Jorge Aquilar held in the General Collection of the Beinecke Rare Book & Manuscript Library at Yale University, and it is used with the library's permission. This type of map, a portolano, concentrates on place names and direction, similar to today's subway map. The back cover uses a section from the same map. And the "waypoint" flag images come from it as well.

Most of the poems' latitude/longitude coordinates were found on https://mynasadata.larc.nasa.gov/latitudelongitude-finder/ and all were confirmed on Google Earth.

Contents

Waypoint [noun \ wā- póint \ ]

: an intermediate point on a route or line of travel, a stopping point or point at which a course is changed, a reference point.

Weathervane

Where you come from,
where you've been—
wind,
I have a way of knowing your name.
Once you catch my attention
I am all yours.
Take me where you're going.

Bordentown Marsh

You put in at Bordentown Beach
next to the Delaware River,
having planned to rise with the tide
up Crosswicks Creek
as far as you can reach,
till it begins to subside, turns,
and delivers you back where you started—
but never back where you began
thinking of the marsh in the summer. See,
where you began is not where you will be.

Stroke by stroke, you paddle past
the yacht club with cabin cruisers
lined up along the pier,
bearing names like *Mezzaluna, Fast
and Furious,* and *Fare Thee Well, My Friend.*
Under the trestle bridge of the light rail line,
the current carries you beyond
Point Breeze, Joseph Bonaparte's
cliff estate, now just a memory.
Here, for our purposes, the marshland starts.

Along the right, stretches of wild rice
Lenape once harvested. To the left,
a maze of waterways beckon,
twisting through the crowding spatterdock

40.147892° N / 74.718318° W

and blue-spiked pickerelweed
and narrowing canyons of rushes.
You are not to be sucked in, I reckon.
Onward, the wider stream flushes
out, with just enough dalliance,
log-sunning turtles before they plunk

from sight. A heron flaps off the bank
in dowager drag. I once followed
a beaver that wanted to be followed,
leading me away from his hangout,
till he dove and I tracked his bubbles.
Then he surfaced and whacked the water
with his broad flat tail, turned about
and ducked beneath the boat and disappeared—
simply dismissing his troubles
with one emphatic statement.

40.147892° N / 74.718318° W

Minnows scatter in bursts
of silver ripples against the shoreline.
The day grows full of festive finds and firsts.
A fish flings itself carelessly
above the water, momentarily
suspended in a brighter, lighter world—
as if to glimpse a life
beyond its lukewarm comfort zone:
this moving palette of green and yellow
and sky blue, pierced with purple loosestrife.

In the lull between the push and pull
of the tide, when the water swirls in
indecision, you can close your eyes
and let the boat float free
to follow the current's consensus
that is never wrong and always a surprise.
Among the cattails and the bulrushes
weaves the *conk-la-ree'* of the red-winged blackbird.
That you'll have to hear yourself.
I'll not say another word.

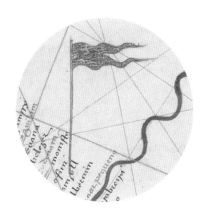

Reaching Inuvik (Northwest Territories)

From Dawson City, the Dempster Highway
carried me for 450 miles
(I was flotsam in its current),
as the car hung to its gravel back
that was racing down, up, and across
the permafrost terrain, through the Tombstone
Mountains, beyond the Arctic Circle,
into the Richardsons, over the Peel
and Mackenzie Rivers, on its route
to Inuvik, like a wild fire hose.

Stunted trees leaned in all directions.
Fog and rain hounded me on a hunt
for the midnight sun. The windshield cracked
from an onslaught of pebbles flung
by the only passing van. Two ravens
reigned at the Arctic Circle boundary,
a raucous, convivial couple
holding court in a vacant parking lot.
They pecked off insects from the car's front grill.
I crowned them Patience and Opportunity.

When I finally rolled into Inuvik,
I wasted no time at the bed and breakfast.
The sled dogs in their cages were calling.
They wanted a walk—more like a dash,

68.360744° N / 133.723018° W

5

as I learned—jerking me forth on the leash.
Then I saw the snow white, blue-eyed puppies,
rowdy rambunctious dwarfs crowding a door.
When I entered, I was rushed at once
by a flurry of soft tender longing:
the welcome party I'd been looking for.

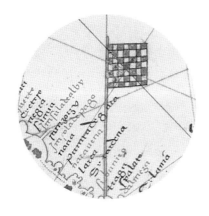

Down upon the Suwannee River
For Patrick Nichols

On Easter Sunday, we loaded
our flotilla of kayaks and canoes
for a week of rapture with our muse.
The moon followed us every night,
from Fargo to Live Oak.
The limestone-powdered beaches,
where we pitched our tents,
were white as bleached bed sheets;
the sculpted rocks along the banks
smelled and echoed like catacombs.

The local forecast
warned of cloudy weather,
with chances of daily rain.
We sweated under the sun,
swam and floated beside our campsites.
Tupelo and cypress trees
waved their Spanish moss
at our silent paddle parade.
'Gators were small in size and number,
else invisible in the tea-colored water.

The river twisted and turned like an itch,
its steady current egging us along.
At Suwannee Springs, where droves in the past

30.681786° N / 82.560099° W

came to cleanse in the sulfur baths,
alone, we scrunched our toes into the sand.
Through the crumbling stone wall window
I watched a snake swim towards me, then concede.
The takeout was nearby, the packing up,
unceremonial: the you, me, we'd . . .
Our group dispersed—puff—like a dandelion.

Thought Trains in Hopewell

Nightly, the thought trains rumble through Hopewell
on rickety track.

Coursing down the rails, herded by a horn's
importuning, cars

sway and jostle, while their undulant sound,
pounding across miles,

approaches and gathers and swarms, pushing
its point through the dark

landscape that absorbs and disperses it,
as the horde drones by

and recedes, dragging a stubborn silence
along the railbed.

In the morning, I vaguely remember
which ones I hopped on.

40.391746° N / 74.76269° W

Victory Point, King William Island

In August, when the zodiacs beached
us on the island, one of the first
things we noticed was also the worst,
mosquitoes that had reached
their zenith in ubiquitous swarm.
At 69° north latitude,
it was surprisingly warm
for expedition jackets: we stewed,

and wandered around swatting the air
with one hand, while zipping, unzipping
with the other. It was an unforgiving
board-flat hell, if I may say so: prayer
stone rejects galore, algae-choked pools,
the encroaching ice pack that
heeded no Admiralty rules.
This clearly was a doormat

where the back of winter wiped its frozen ass.
I quickly took some photos: the troops
were hastening back like nincompoops
to the icebreaker lazing offshore. But, yes,
sadly, it was here Sir John Franklin's men
came, abandoning their ships to the ice
where they'd been trapped in a tightening vise
grip for eighteen months. They built a cairn,

69.666666° N / 98.309248° W

scrawled a note, then stoically trudged
into oblivion. Several dozen
search vessels, devoting years, misjudged
the ships' itinerary; the world was stunned
by the tragic toll. As solace, perhaps,
the Arctic now is better known on maps:
each island, strait, and inlet bears a name
(an English nobleman's, of course). Claimed fame.

One day when we all disappear,
go missing, get irretrievably lost—
as on this vast horizonless bier—
it would be nice to hope (could we trust?)
that something significant will be found
by those who follow our footsteps to trample
over the same haunted ground:
a Northwest Passage, for example.

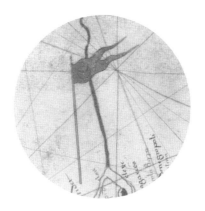

Summer Band

Chetzemoka Park, Port Townsend

With their lawn chairs and wide-brimmed hats,
spreading blankets and picnic baskets—
some with walkers, one with oxygen tank—
the crowd assembles in puzzle pieces
before the gazebo, where brass instruments,
horns and percussion, the chopsticks of the drummer,
all wait for the conductor's baton
to release the oracle of summer.

JIZAAM—and with that the fanfare unfolds:
some military marches, selections
from Broadway hits, the obligatory
Sousa. No one could be disappointed.
Children climb shade-bearing trees, frisbees
tease scampering dogs. The band grand slams.
At water's edge, among seaweeded rocks,
low-tide beachcombers scavenging for clams

draw us to the bay, where lustrous sharp sails
seamlessly slice the fabric of the air.
For an hour the puzzle is complete:
boisterous sound, the grateful audience,
a soothing breeze beneath a cloudless sky.
The music is both factor and locus
for an afternoon of light existence

48.122674° N / 122.755308° W

when age and time drift out of focus.

Afterwards, a gradual breaking up,
an unvoiced unanimous agreement
to gather again whenever we can
for another tuneful summer séance.
All the while, in panted exhalations
of pure oxygen (oh Great Beholder!),
my neighbor's breathing machine affirms:

We all will get old, but never older.

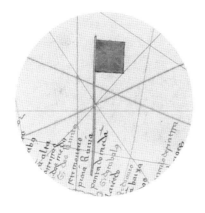

48.122674° N / 122.755308° W

HikeCoo-ing to Machu Picchu

Posthaste from Lima—
into the interior
on wonder's wingspan.

13.163141° S / 72.544963° W

High expectations:
Inca capital, Cusco,
colonial town.

Christian festival
hoists Spanish conquistador:
burdensome idols.

13.163141° S / 72.544963° W

Street inquisitions:
masked whipping boys raising welts
on Corpus Christi.

Sacsayhuamàn (say
'sexy woman'): stone stronghold,
now Humpty Dumpty.

Skirted in thin air,
Salkantay's sacred summit
catches our deep breaths.

My cocoa leaf prayer:
may you sharpen your senses
along the knife edge.

Clouds claim the mountain—
still we climb in its presence:
altitude addicts.

Crossed over the past—
and found a sunlit future's
unfolding present.

The way the river
favors the valley's floor, our
trail turns the mountain.

When we got a glimpse,
the goose bumps began to jump
between now and then.

Mystic morning rite:
interpreting the silence
of Machu Picchu.

Terraces of time,
where oblivious llamas
graze among clouds.

Daft dandelion
to the ancient stonework said:
"Make a wish and blow."

"Widen the window."
The transcendental tourist
sees ruins recede.

Up these Inca stairs
rushed 500 footstepped years.
I will take my time.

13.163141° S / 72.544963° W

Guide me to the hut
at the top of the mountain
where the gods hang out.

Christmas Dinner, 1965

Simsbury, Connecticut

Taken after dinner, before dessert,
the chairs pushed back, our bellies full:
my father, my grandmother, two brothers-in-law,
my three sisters, three toddlers, and me.
Only two are facing the camera.
The youngest, in a high chair, reaches out
for the table, or is about to drop
something—the resolution isn't clear—
but she's captured everyone's attention.
(A grownup now, with children of her own.)

My grandmother, looking lost, disapproves.
I never saw her smile or heard her laugh.
She presents a sullen face. The others
engage, react, seem almost comfortable
in their dress shirts and holiday outfits:
still hard to believe they'd all get divorced,
my parents, too, some years before they died.
One brother-in-law would cut his life short.
I turn my head back, over my shoulder,
agreeing to be included, lips sealed.

But now let me speak for the group of us,
offering our grateful hearts to the one
who cooked the meal and, dropping her napkin

on the table's corner, jumped up to snap
this most impromptu family picture,
where sitting all together one last time—
the green tablecloth, the lit red candles,
a centerpiece of pine cones and oak leaves,
the pine-paneled room and ashless fireplace—
we inhabit her love. On the mantel,

ceramic candle letters spell NOEL.

Darwin Road

The dead fox was hard to explain,
despite being so close to Death Valley.
There it lay, bloodless, in the road
that severed two desert distances.
How could one choose which way to go?
Outwitted, I wasn't that curious.

On both sides, Joshua Trees stood,
posing with their pumped-up arms
like body-builders wearing boxing gloves.
The heat was pummeling the glass.
Sparring, I swung the rental car
around. The tires' flight was furious.

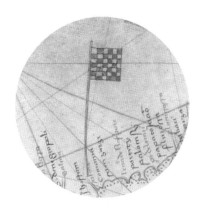

Villa Ukika

The last native Yaghan speaker
lives in a cluster
of modest cottages
outside Puerto Williams
on the Beagle Channel.
When I went to visit, hoping
to hear the sharp guttural sounds
of this dying language,
the tourist season had ended;
the cultural shop was closed.
I peered through the window
at the handmade canoes
and knitted woolens,
the crafted apparatus
that sustains the site.
Dogs were gathering for dinner
as I started back to my room
in a rabid snow squall.

At the uttermost end of the earth,
in Magellan's Land of Fire,
through which Darwin passed
on his querying voyage,
the natural selection of language
continues its work in whispers—
not because no one speaks

54.933297° S / 67.591161° W

the tongue, for one still does,
at least during the summer months.
Gone are the listeners.

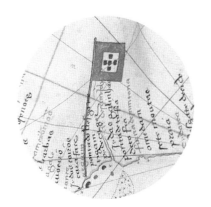

Walking on Wargo

It's a rural road deer dart across
to reach their familiar paths through the fields
and the woods. I live over there, not far.
Houses cling to one side, petering out
as the road narrows and turns, angling by
the pond where Canadian geese re-group
now and then and swans are sometimes sighted
drifting above the dam and its intake grate.
People leave their cars here to fish or hike.

Around the bend, the CSA farmhouse
and its rustic red barn serve welcome
to the passersby or those picking up
their weekly share of harvested crops.
Children hide and seek beside the office.
In field after field, mounded rows advance
in parallel, plants sprouting from plastic—
beans and berries, my favorite lettuce.
Where the road meets Titus Mill, I turn back.

It's where you take a long walk after work.
Where you choose to head out the day after
your husband dies in bed—as I once met
a neighbor on a late spring afternoon.
Song birds evervesced through the foliage.
Everything was maddening green and gold

against the sky.
           Where, after Parkinson's
has claimed your companion, you go to breathe
in the consoling smell of country air
before returning to the dreaded business
of a life that had been tolerable, yet safe,
for so many years, and now isn't there.

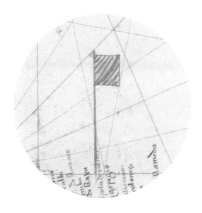

40.359618° N / 74.76331° W

General Sherman Tree

*"The General Sherman Tree . . . is the largest (by volume) tree in the
world" (National Park Service, Sequoia National Park, California).*

Born before Christ, you have lived longer
than most idolatries. Let us pray
to your tower of ever-growing glory,
and learn from your ring-written story
how life ascends every day
towards the heavens: ever stronger,

more deeply rooted, and distinct.
You're also older than most countries—how
many crowns have fallen since?—and still
you stand and increase your breadth. Will
you accept me as your citizen now,
before everything below becomes extinct?

Your state of being is immobile.
Our frantic days swirl hourless around
your base: time must trespass in your kingdom.
Please consider me a faithful pilgrim
who, sheltered briefly in your presence, found
solace in something naturally noble.

36.581656° N / 118.751442° W

Long Lights in Brooklyn

My father was born on Hancock Street
in the ground floor unit of a two-story house.
Instead, we found an apartment building,
its lower windows grilled with iron bars.
The city block was choked with parked cars,
and tired trees were dropping their fall leaves.

Sleuthing the old family addresses
recovered more familiar distresses:
spaces overcrowded, sounds discordant,
a worn environment, a gradual
degradation (overstimulation)
of senses. Strident, impoverished places.

Gumball-yellow school buses bubbled out
small children wearing backpacks—toy soldiers,
I thought, embarking on take-home missions.
Shoppers with styrofoam-filled plastic bags
carried Chinese food or hot chicken wings,
clothes emblazoned with pop-culture logos.

We sat a long time at the traffic lights,
wondering where everyone was destined
as they hustled by on the sidewalks,
hunkered under sweatshirt hoods, enraptured
in their headphone music or cellphone texts.

This Flatbush future I never questioned.

My mother's girlhood home had an open,
unscreened window. I watched a teenage girl
slip inside the white door, bruised and blackened.
I wanted to wish her the best of luck.
Wires hung down where porch lights had been.
A tree stood sentry above a brand new getaway truck.

Would the past always seem more hopeful
and gracious till the Depression came?
A Wurlitzer world of vaudeville skits
and matinees at the Kings (so regal!)—
over ice cream sodas thinking out loud
how swell life was. Then pop went the weasel.

Notes on Trekking to Makalu Base Camp, Nepal

"Say goodbye to there, hello to here." —advice of Ram,
our group's Sirdar

We flew on Cosmic Air
to Biratnagar,
far east and south of Kathmandu:
wore cotton ear plugs
and sipped on soda,
glimpsing Everest
before dropping down
to a two-way landing strip.

Met porters and mountains
of gear. A six-hour bus ride
to camp above Basantapur:
huge swaybacks, sheer drops,
terraced hills. An unpaved road.
Fog and light rain at 7500 feet.
Dinner of dal bhat, bananas and beans.
Seven of us, four tents. Dogs bark all night.

The rock trails begin
with a train of *dzos* passing through.
A mother and daughter flip-flop
up with sacks of rice on their backs.
Chapatis and yak cheese for lunch.
Camped at Chauki, an open plain;
heavy rain through the night. Makeshift
kitchen ringed by village children.

27.807410° N / 87.078668° E

Porridge for breakfast, crosslegged
on tarp. Donated rupees to school
we passed. Kids' "Namaste" greeting.
Rhododendron forests. Porters
holding umbrellas, listening
to Indian music. Ram Pokhari
camp on hillside near five-building town.
Heavy rain again at night.

Our wake-up call at 6 a.m.
with tea and biscuits at tent door.
Head and Shoulders shampoo
in store, handkerchiefs bright
with *Titanic* film stars.
Cows coming down the trail.
A local woman sells beans to our cook.
A terrain of terraced rice paddies.

Toilet tent set up next to tombs.
Dinner by candlelight on porch.
A two-leech day, three-pee night.
Suspension bridges to cross.
Piluna Khola: torrential rain
(a theme) at night. Bamboo stands,
field girls cutting greens
for their animals. Our Peter,

a pied piper to the wide-eyed children.
Headache from iodine in the water?
Camp on little-used trail section;
rain pouring again at night.
Rains most of the day. We hike overgrown
paths, stepping through streams on boulders.

Parts of flip-flops the only trail trash.
One village phone: chance to call home.

Our procession descends on small town
like entering medieval France;
offered someone's house. Light night rain
continues in the morning.
Filling our bottles with filtered water
attracts much local interest.
Houses on stilts in the paddies:
animals below, people space above.

Following the Sabha Khola river,
unattended fishing poles,
a suspension bridge. Swimming
in the river but no soap allowed.
Candlelight dinner by the water,
no bugs, some stars, porters singing, dancing.
Another day. A woman threshing
rice with her feet. A primary school:

children with bright white shirts, blue pants,
boys playing soccer with a fruit ball.
We climb on stone steps, up all day,
and camp in a leech-field among cattle,
foreheads bleeding. They gravitate
to a central rock to rub the pests off.
Up early, we soon reach the main trail;
Num (rhymes with "doom") is our destination.

Maoist village. A private English school
with dirt-floor schoolroom. We provide
pronunciation reading some pages.

27.807410° N / 87.078668° E

"God bless everything," kids recite,
lining up outside for dismissal, then
scooting away in their crimson and white.
Dinner on porch out of the rain
and the dark. Rain continued all night.

We cross the raging Arun River
3000 feet down from Num,
then climb 3000 feet up
on trails centuries old, made of rock,
impervious to the teeming sky.
Dried out in Sedua at Makulu Lodge.
Now have entered the Makulu-Barun
National Park. Kami cooks banana pie!

Village dog barked for hours last night;
counted 100 barks per minute,
on what diet? Cotton shirts still wet.
There is no top of the hill in Nepal,
always another, looming beyond it.
Passed *mani* wall with Buddhist mantras,
child wearing a training basket.
Reach Tashigaon. Camp at 7000 feet,

above town, on a precipice
overlooking the vast valley, peaks
in the distance. At 7 a.m.,
porters have last smoke before leaving.
Log-crossing stream, herd of mountain sheep
flowing down the trail, a barefoot shepherd
carrying a lamb, calves following *dzos*.
Heard a deer coughing in the woods.

Most difficult climb, often using hands,
rock by rock. Reach Kongma,
another 5000 feet up,
weather clearing, views of peaks.
Leech on my hand during the night,
blood over everything. Prayer flags
with *chorten*. Dobato, rhododendron
valley, steep descent of 1000 feet

in the morning. One misstep, trek over.
Follow sherpa for hours in silence.
Arrive at Yangre Kharkha (12,000 feet),
past stone *gompa*, in wide meadow
with Barun River running through it,
huge cliffs opposite. Four o'clock tea
carried on trays from a stone kitchen.
Have yet to see Mount Makalu.

We head north along Barun River Valley,
alpine meadows in fall color,
waterfalls abound. White peaks in glory.
Meet another herd of sheep, then
a yak-led group of *dzos*.
Past treeline, we stop at Yak Karkha
(14,500 feet) early,
to acclimate. Clouds over. Rain at night.

First morning challenge: crossing raging stream
on log. Occasional snow flurries.
Moraine formed by Barun Glacier.
Trail climbs in sand and scree beside the flow.
Reach Shershong at 15,500 feet.

27.807410° N / 87.078668° E

Lunch in view of massive Peak 6.
Two days here. Hiked up the valley
for our first view of god Makalu,

fifth highest mountain in the world.
Robed in white, broad-shouldered vestments.
Shaped like a four-sided pyramid.
Light so bright, I squint in sunglasses.
A satisfaction that surpasses what?
Healthy, strong; another challenge, ready.
October 11, 2001.
A man-made calendar still to climb.

A beautiful morning, best yet, no wind.
Engulfing quiet. Clamber up
a steep ridge with Larry and sherpa
to catch sight of Everest, Lhotse.
Transitory, capricious clouds.
Guess 17,500 feet.
Barun Pokhari Lake below. Lay awake
to sleet and avalanche rumblings.

Tents covered in white in the morning.
We begin the long return, following
our footsteps, crossing Shipton La Pass.
Young children minding cows, a woman
sifting rice on top of a large flat rock.
Harvested rice paddies. We greet
a Japanese group heading north,
listening to country western music;

a large Dutch troop with tables and chairs.
A fortnight bazaar in Sedua,
tailors using hand-driven sewing machines,

girls trying nail polish, trinket trading.
Our typical candlelight dinner.
Cows collect at public water tap;
I take a body wash and draw a crowd.
Clear views of mountains from where we had come,

as if we had climbed blindfolded:
all now revealed. Increase of oxygen
noticeable and appreciated.
A woman in her garden before seven.
Pass Chichila, children playing hopscotch.
More trail traffic, rock piles for trail repair.
Suzanne calls Ram a leprechaun:
his disappearing act, triangle hat.

Pass Bhote Bash. A lovely bamboo fence.
We decide on our tips for the staff.
In Khandbari, a Khukuri knife workshop.
A dead goat's head washed in a bucket.
View of Tumlingtar town and airport.
Beer at last. Last trek dinner in camp:
porters and locals, with flute and drum,
sing and dance. It rains at night: *de jure.*

Walk to airport on narrow dirt path;
sit in grass fifty yards from the plane,
waiting for pilot's return from lunch.
The Cosmic Air prop
rests like an anachronism
to carry us back to Kathmandu—
a grateful, faithful seven
to a post-9/11 world.

Already far from that heaven.

27.807410° N / 87.078668° E

Saturday Night on Thursday Island
(Torres Strait)

The wind continues at twenty knots.
The tide is out along the esplanade.
Locals loiter in sheltered spots.
Prone in bed, I pray for Scheherazade.

Prone in bed, I pray for Scheherazade
to spin me stories throughout the night.
My mind is even, my feeling's odd.
Above, the fan puts up a frantic fight.

Above, the fan puts up a frantic fight
against marauding mobs of clammy air—
its scimitars whirling left and right
as if the dark spawns demons everywhere.

As if the dark spawns demons everywhere,
I'm desperate to achieve some piece of sleep—
below the surface of this watery lair
to become a pearl diver of the deep.

To become a pearl diver of the deep,
I close my eyes. I hold my breath. The plots
thicken in the murk about. Senses creep.
The whirling dervish wind ties time in knots.

I blow the genie out.

Ka'awa Loa Lanai

I think I will wait here
till the next mango falls,
enjoying the breeze above
the repercussions
of Kealakekua Bay
where Captain Cook fell
from a stab in the back
more than two centuries ago.
A resident gecko
slurps the papaya juice
left in my cocktail glass.
From here, the lawn drops off
more than a thousand feet.
One could paraglide down
to Pu'uhonua o Honaunau,
the ancient safehaven
for miscreants and sinners.
Let the guestbook show how
I dillydallied here
while wistful thoughts
crossed my mind
on their way down
to the white oblivion
beach where I'm headed.

There's a loud crashing now
through the leaves of the tree.
With a thud the ripe fruit lands.
Time to go.

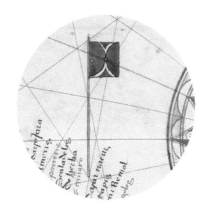

The Manse (glass plate negative, circa 1885)
427 Polk Street, Port Townsend, Washington

We only see the positive from this negative:
the original is too fragile.
In it, I meet the first tenants
of the house where I now live.

An all-stone church stands guard to the right,
boasting a new bell tower.
The two homes form a pair, inseparable,
like body and mind, grit and spirit.

Mrs. Reid sits reading at the end of the porch,
in floor-length Victorian dress.
Reverend Reid, in waistcoat, stands
leaning on the middle post, clutching papers—

probably called out from his study
when the photographer arrived.
Perhaps he was working on a sermon,
thinking of the soul's salvation.

He looks distracted by the horizon.
Their little girl, out in the dirt street,
clutches her doll tightly and turns
in her sun hat to face the camera.

48.115113° N / 122.759981° W

An unknown young man, not their son,
slumps against the porch wall, his hands
in his pockets, questioning his role.
Curly corbels trimming the porch's posts—

an oversize bay window on the side—
several newly-planted trees, enclosed
in laddered wooden pyramids,
challenging the horse-drawn wagons—

the picket fence, unbroken to the church.
Such are the lost details of this landscape
viewed from a lens on a tripod—
praise be to God—unblemished as time.

I found the Reids' grave in Laurel Grove,
marked with a flat stone (and no epitaph),
including the name of Baby Roy,
who died before he could be saved
by this archival photograph.

48.115113° N / 122.759981° W

Rounding Cape Horn

Below 40 degrees south there is no law.
Below 50 degrees there is no god. —*old sailors' saw*

Our engine couldn't reverse;
the mainsail was torn:
we decided to skirt
the island counterclockwise.
If we tried to dock
at the albatross monument
dedicated to lost mariners,
we'd probably get stuck
ourselves. It was not worth
pushing our luck
in the clouding weather
with the sea and wind rising.
Tacking west, we slingshot past
the northwest shoulder
and quickly were racing
south towards Drake's Passage
and Antarctica.
The view vacated
into a lost horizon;
the boat stiffly listed,
reaching across the wind
on the rolling waves.
A gradual turn of the wheel
to port and the tension

55.983333° S / 67.266667° W

eased, and the boat
began to fly. There it was:
the massive rock face
of the Horn's cliff,
looming above us
in ridges green and gray—
where a thousand ships
paid their last respects
before the grave.
"But not us today."

Now we were running before the wind and the waves,
lifting on the water like an exclamation.

Kilimanjaro*

There's only one way to reach the top:
pole-pole (which translates as "slowly").
On our way up, we passed some trekkers,
who had risked the migraine/vomit route,
coming down in an uncontrolled gallop.

I followed my son's headlamp in the dark,
up the endless switchbacks, led by Peter.
The sun met us warmly at Gilman's Point.
Then we trudged for another hour
or two before gaining Uhuru's mark

in the clearing morning light. The icefields
loomed vast and lovely, blue and white, the crater
far below—Mawenzi poking through the clouds,
not to be forgotten. There was nothing
we hadn't climbed above: thus the dream yields

to the fact of an all-encompassing view.
I needed to catch my breath, to remove
the layers I wouldn't wear going down.
"Dad, we need to take the pictures over,
with the leis"—given at Marangu

to vouchsafe our journey on the mountain.
Through rain forest, moorland, alpine desert,

3.076388° S / 37.354229° E

we acclimated to achieve Kibo's
arctic. We'll need to scale this life again—
pole-pole. It rhymes with holy.

---

*At 19,340 feet, Kilimanjaro is the highest mountain in
Africa. Our climb took six days; on the seventh we rested.

Kayaking on the South Branch
of the Raritan River
For Gino Gentile

The rural branch of the river
eased past us in the light rain
as we slid our kayaks over the sand
into the clear water, and lowered
ourselves in at Three Bridges.
Soon, fields of corn, stands of wild rice
framed our gentle meandering.
The sun came out and looked us over.
In a wading area under a bridge,
kids were swimming and shrieking,
but stopped everything to watch
us pass in a few strong strokes.
Just around another bend,
we came upon a plastic beach ball
bearing a young girl's face,
like a princess, with decals
of toy animals, floating
indolently downstream.
I imagined Lenape Indians
fishing on the riverbank
centuries ago, watching
this ball stray into view. What
would they have thought? How

would their cosmos have changed? Or,
maybe they would have turned their tasks
to cleaning fish, just as it drifted by.

Dinner at the Dardanelles
(Çanakkale, Turkey)

For my sister Carol

Families were strolling along the quay,
if you remember; there was a cool breeze.
We had just come back from Gallipoli—
from a day-long tour of modern madness
that, over dinner, left a lot to say.

I had in my pocket a slender smooth stone
from Anzac Cove that I rolled in my hand.
I planned to add it to the one from Troy,
which we had visited the day before:
collecting what a young boy would have thrown.

The spector of Hector and Achilles
clanging and slashing before the grand gate,
scuffing up dust that still clouds history,
hung over the trenches and the beaches
we saw, I think. I still love feta cheese.

I forget what else we ate—some Turkish
delight, I'm sure, as you had insisted:
"You don't travel abroad to be foolish"
and act as if you had never left home.
My appetite was hungry for the sites,

40.150199° N / 26.401995° E

husbands holding hands with their head-scarfed wives,
children trailing along in vests and shorts,
putting their best-dressed figures forward
on a Friday night. Such innocent airs.
Something of custom and comfort survives

even in the most unlikely places.
Where someone died is now a monument.
Perhaps there is a restaurant next door
or a money-changing business. The smell
of pastry and spices slowly erases

any old lingering traces. We live:
the present and past jostling each other
like siblings for control. "It's mine / it's mine."
The obligatory bench says, "Sit down.
Take a moment to be contemplative."

In the Greek myth, Hero waited with her lamp
for Leander to begin his nightly
crossing. A winter wind snuffed its light out.
She added her death to his drowning.
Over all rolls time's indelible stamp.

Troy is miles from Aegean beaches now:
river sediment has broadened the fields,
as we layer memories of youth
upon those of Homer and the ancients,

getting ever farther from the soil, truth.

An endless line of container ships and such
paraded through the strait as we drank tea.
It was where Byron swam the Hellespont!
Constantinople is now Istanbul.
Age changes us we think, but not that much.

Why

We are all looking for a place to die
while we live. May the choice be up to you.
Does it take a lifetime to say goodbye?

There are jobs to learn, and many will try
to make them the work that they want to do
while they are looking for a place to die.

And there are roles to play, like girl and guy,
where love and chemistry determine who
could take a lifetime to say goodbye.

In one woman's arms I found the peace to cry,
and felt that all my tracking might be through,
as I was looking for a place to die.

Believe what you want, but not the cruel lie
that, deepest down, sounds too good to be true,
says life will take its time *after* goodbye.

This is our resting place: beneath the sky
and its wishful stars and wild yonder blue.
Look, we are all dying to answer why
life is the time we take to say goodbye.

Where

My mother died at Hospice Savannah,
1352 Eisenhower Drive—
barely three miles from where, in the 40s,
she had begun to raise our family.

What makes it strange to me, and uncanny,
is the idea that she must have driven
many times down Skidaway, past Derenne,
not ever thinking there would be the spot,
among the towering pines and live oak,
where her spirit would find rest in fifty years.

My parents moved fifteen times, mostly north,
before they settled down in Simsbury,
Connecticut, where I grew up. Divorced,
my mother vowed to see the world, taking
passage on cargo ships, smoking in peace.
I guess Savannah always tugged at her.

But as a young wife, passing by those woods
during many hot and humid summer days
so long ago, what if she could have known
they'd be developed for her final home?
Would she have turned her head? Stopped a moment
to stroll beneath the Spanish moss and cry?

32.005039° N / 81.092153° W

To smoke a cigarette, then stub it out,
toeing the sandy soil with its ashes?
So I stand in the hospice parking lot,
watching my mother drive heedlessly by.

———

I don't know why
I need to know
where I will die.
But here, there—
I go looking.

Statement about *Waypoints*

Many of the poems I write seem to be associated with places, which has made me think of them as "waypoints." When you hike today with a GPS system, you can set waypoints so as to later review the twists and turns and elevations of the journey. Perhaps it's not so difficult to think that the same role holds true with poems. My poetic fascination with place goes way back, probably to my first reading of, and astonishment at, William Wordsworth's "Lines Composed a Few Miles above Tintern Abbey, On Revisiting the Banks of the Wye during a Tour. July 13, 1798." *Waypoints* is my first collection.

JOHN DELANEY recently retired after 35 years in the Dept. of Rare Books and Special Collections of Princeton University Library, where he was head of manuscripts processing and then, for the last 15 years, curator of historic maps. He has written a number of works on cartography, including *Strait Through: Magellan to Cook and the Pacific; First X, Then Y, Now Z: An Introduction to Landmark Thematic Maps;* and *Nova Caesarea: A Cartographic Record of the Garden State, 1666-1888.* These have extensive website versions. He has written poems for most of his life, and, in the 1970s, he attended the Writing Program of Syracuse University, where his mentors were poets W. D. Snodgrass and Philip Booth. No doubt, in subtle ways, they have bookended his approach to poems. John has traveled widely, preferring remote, natural settings, and is addicted to kayaking and hiking.